Raspberry Pi 2 User Guide

Learn How It Works and Create 25 Fun & Easy Raspberry Pi Projects

Table of contents

Introduction

We all love geniuses and heroes. So you want to be that imagined genius or hero? Raspberry Pi 2 presents you with an environment to build your first robot, an opportunity to learn programmatic thinking skills, beyond just hardware hacking and simple coding. This little board literally holds the future for modern electronics.

A good number of today's computing devices are locked down to support only a few operations. Operations only envisaged by the manufacturer and not YOU. With such closed platforms, you can only experiment your creative thoughts up to some point, beyond which you become entrapped by hardware support issues, and your thought processes prematurely halt.

With all these barriers in sight, Raspberry Pi, an inexpensive, high-performing hardware was launched with amazing 3D graphics capability, memory, and support for general purpose programming. This device is popular with experimenters, inventors, hackers, and tinkerers.

Early Pi models would run on several versions of Linux, including Arch Linux, Fedora Remix, and Debian, thanks to porting, which allows you to alter original code to fit individual distributions.

Technical specifications of Pi 2

The processor and memory upgrade on RP2 implies more performance than what we experienced with earlier models. RP2 comes with the following features:

o   BCM 2836 ARM, v7 quad-core processor (900MHz): a powerful core with 4 processors

o   1 GB RAM and 40 pin GPIO

o   4 USB ports (2.0)

o   CSI connector and DSI connector

o   Ethernet port

o   HDMI port

o   Micro SD port

o   3.5 mm audio jack and composite video port

o   Micro USB port acting as the power source

Chapter 1 – Installation

Before you plunge yourself into the practical aspects of building your own programs, media center, file server, or web kiosk, you first have to set up your Raspberry PI 2. To set up your RP2 for the very first time, you'll need a number of accessories, including:

o   A standard USB keyboard: You'll find this absolutely necessary if you plan to use your RP2 as a PC. You don't have to change this keyboard in future.

o   A mouse: You will need the mouse more often if you're using your Pi as a desktop computer. If you are using your PI as a server, you might not need the mouse as much.

o   Micro SD card: The Pi that you just acquired runs on some software—the operating system. You need an SD card (at least 8GB) to install this OS.

o   Wi-Fi dongle: You might not need a Wi-Fi dongle if you are comfortable working with an Ethernet cable. You however need this dongle if you intend to connect your Raspberry PI to the Internet wirelessly.

o   Bluetooth dongle: If you intend to pair your Raspberry PI with game controllers, a Bluetooth dongle may be appropriate. This is not particularly essential during the initial setup.

o   RP2 Case: You don't want to see cables protruding all over especially if you are using your PI as some media center, but you'll not need it if you plan to connect to breadboards. Find one with an inbuilt heat sink.

o   Power supply: Find a designated power supply for your RP2.

o   Powered USB hub: Whatever device you plug into the RP2's USB ports consumes power. A powered hub ensures that your PI doesn't crash when serving more Bluetooth dongles.

To get started the easy way, you can purchase a starter kit for your RPI2. A starter kit preempts cases of unsupported input devices or output devices. Such starter kits include Canakit, Vilros, Make, Sunfounder, Adafruit, and many others.

Most of these starter kits come with the items mentioned above, plus a breadboard, user guide, GPIO breakout connector, an assortment of LEDs, and of course the Pi.

How to get started with your RPI2

Once you have gathered all the aforementioned items, it will be time to install NOOBS on your SD card, but first, you need to prepare your SD card.

Insert your micro SD into the card reader on your computer, and format it. It's only then that you can now install NOOBS on the card. If your card came with NOOBS preinstalled, skip this section. Wondering what NOOBS is? NOOBS is the short form for "New Out Of Box Software".

Installing NOOBS

1. Download the NOOBs zip file from https://www.raspberrypi.org/downloads/ and unpack the file on the SD card that you formatted in the previous section. To download the installer, choose between the Offline installer (NOOBS) and the online installer (NOOBS LITE)

2. Copy the contents you extracted in step 1 to the micro SD card

3. Safely eject the micro SD card from your PC and plug it into your RPI2

4. Plug in your monitor, keyboard, and the mouse to help you navigate NOOBS interface. Be sure to turn on the monitor.

5. Power up your RPI2

Installing your choice OS

6. Once you attach the power cable to the Pi, the RPI2 device boots and a display screen shows up with a boot menu.

7. From the list of operating systems, choose the OS that you would want to run on your RPI2.

8. Check the box next to the OS you want to install. This could be Raspbian, Archlinux, OpenELEC, Pidora, RaspBMC, and RiscOS.

9. Click on the **Install** button located on the toolbar to complete installation

Note: RPI2 supports composite video, DSI video, and HDMI video.

If you installed a single operating system, your RPI2 device boots automatically every time you power it on . If you have multiple operating systems installed, a boot selector is displayed when you reboot your device. Holding down the "Shift" key as you reboot redirects you to the installation screen from where you can change your booting options.

Tip: The NOOBS image makes the initial setup of your RP2 easier. With NOOBS installed, you do not have to download any imaging software; the entire process of setting up your RP2 becomes pretty straightforward. NOOBS allows you to install your favorite OS with just one click. You can also install more than one OS

Logging in for the first time

Wait until your Pi boots to completion.

To access the graphical user interface of your Pi, you need to log in with a username (pi) and password (raspberry). When the login prompt appears, enter your username and password: Pi and raspberry are the default username and password respectively.

To load your GUI, simply type the command **startx**

Press **Enter**

Note: As you type in your password, you'll not be able to see any characters on the screen. Both the password and username are in lower case.

Chapter 2 – Quick User Guide

How to install a web browser

We all love big-screen surfing, with your home media center running, it's also possible to add a browser to your media center. All you need to do is install an add-on of your choice browser to your system.

Once you have downloaded the add-on, installing it on OpenElec is easy. Simply click on **System**, and select **Add-ons**. Click on **Install from the zip** and browse for your file.

After installation, reboot your computer.

Alternatively, since you already have a monitor or TV attached to your Pi, you can simply start a terminal, and type this command: **sudo apt- get install chromium-browser**, if you wish to install a Chromium browser.

How to add plug-ins to your menu

Now that you have set up your home media center, it's time to customize its look and feel. Adding favorites to your menu makes it even more user-friendly. To add a favorite plug-in to your menu, click on **System**, and tap on **Skin**; hit **Customizers**, and choose **Main menu item customizer**. Go to **Custom 1** and select **Favorite**. Pick your favorite plug-in and add it to your menu.

How to Automate your Home

In an era where automation comes first before anything else, home automation is something you probably want to try with your new RPI2. Take advantage of the Pi's GPIO pins to transform your home into some digital space.

You can build a web app to switch your lights on or off. One product that you can add to your kit to make that happen is the PiFace. PiFace is an input board that presents you with a safer way of hooking additional digital components to your Pi.

With this device, you can control your living room fan, washing machines, exit doors, lighting, and many other things using relay circuits. Instead of relying on a remote control, think about how you can use the GPIO pins to emulate buttons of your remote control.

Chapter 3 – Create 25 Fun and Easy Raspberry Pi 2 Projects

The RPI2 is a powerful pocket computer that you can use to build a thousand projects. It can be likened to that universal toy that fits every situation. It has the capability of the normal PC, but is awesomely affordable since it doesn't feature unnecessary components associated with ordinary computers.

It doesn't come with a case, mouse, monitor, or keyboard, unless if you purchased it as part of a starter kit. It's small, compact, and mobile making it the preferred tool of trade for tinkerers and experimenters. Despite its peculiarly small size, the RPI2 remains persistently big for creating fun projects, other than just learning how to program.

1. Building a home media center

The easiest project that you can build with your Pi, and perhaps your first project, is a living room media center. You can call it anything, living room PC, home PC, or mini media center. With Kodi (XBMC) installed on your device, simply hook up your TV to the Pi to get started straightaway. Kodi is open-source software that allows you to play back videos and other digital media files on the Internet or your local network.

Using this software, you can build an interactive media center with your RPI2 and enjoy high-fidelity Netflix streaming, live-TV streaming, and music streaming. With the RPI2 media center running, you can stream podcasts and other media on HBO GO, Hulu, and many other services. You can even record live TV shows and other video to watch them offline on your local network, thanks to the PVR capabilities of Kodi. If you intend to build something that's more functional, you may want to buy some remote control.

Follow the installation procedure mentioned in an earlier section to install OpenELEC. Use the NOOBS image to install OpenElec. It's easy; all you need to do is follow the onscreen directions to have your software running.

To install your Kodi media center (entertainment center), download the latest version of Kodi from Kodi.tv. For those with older versions of XBMC, simply overwrite the old version with the newer version.

Experiment different ways of turning your TV into a smart TV.

2. Building a Pi case

Raspberry Pi is offered at a very low cost, probably because it doesn't come with all the conventional parts of an ordinary computer. You Pi comes stripped down almost to the core, without a monitor and numerous other parts to allow you to experiment with just as much if modern electronics is something you enjoy.

The board comes naked without even a case, a good window for you to build your own case. If you are an experimenter, you wouldn't waste an extra dollar buying a plastic case or any other case if you can build one.

You don't have to be accurate; try out different styles and materials. Make sure you cleave openings for all the ports, and another one to act as a vent.

3. Building a Retro Gaming Console

At some point in our lives, we've all enjoyed computer games, and it behaves us to make the entire gaming experience even better and more memorable with our own inventions.

Using additional components, like joysticks and buttons, you can actually use your RPI2 to build a Retro gaming console. For instance, Adafruit sells a number of components that you can connect to your Pi to construct a hand-held gaming device that's well portable. Call it PortaBerry Pi.

4. Building a weather station

Other than relying on TV weather forecasts to monitor what's happening around you, you can build your own weather station using the RPI2 device. Make your Raspberry Pi weather station as customized as possible to capture what's only of interest to you. Get all the alerts that matter to you about temperature, humidity, rain, pressure, wind direction, and much more right on your home server.

5. Building an RPI2 Supercomputer

No tinkerer would have thought of building a supercomputer from traditional components without a sponsor or huge financial outlay. With the advent of the Pi, you can now combine more than one RPI2 board to build a powerful supercomputer at just $2000 or even less. The performance power of a single RPI2 is compared to that of a Pentium II.

When you have a cluster of RPI2's working together, the overall workload reduces and performance improves. The Pi should be the first thing that comes to your mind when you think of DIY computing. With support from this magical computer board, you can assemble only the most useful components at the least cost, and leverage their combined power to build a device bigger than the individual components.

And that's how you build a supercomputer for so little. Think of how you can hook up a number of Pi's to leverage their aggregate power. If you really want to make the best out of distributed computing, RPI2 promises just as much.

6. Building a bitTorrent RPI2 server

The Raspberry Pi 2 is a powerful computing device with unlimited applications, and one way you can tap into its unbounded power is to build your own torrent machine. All you'll need is a working RPI2, Internet connection, and SD card.

7. Building a KindleBerry Pi

Most programmers will be contented with minimalistic design, and having a kindle play as your Raspberry monitor (call it KindleBerry Pi) instead of your TV is definitely something you would want to try out. This can be done with a little jail breaking of your kindle. Once you have your KindleBerry screen, connect it to the RPI2 using a USB cable. This would be much easier if you have some prior knowledge in security penetration.

8. Building an improvised keyboard

Ever thought of a working keyboard made up of entirely beer cans? Perhaps it's time you thought of such a keyboard for your RPI2. With an additional board like the Arduino board, it's actually possible to build a keyboard with numerous beer cans as your keys.

9. Building RPI2 cloud server

The raspberry Pi 2 gives you a powerful platform to build a custom, private cloud at incredibly low cost. A few years ago, you'd be comfortable sharing a PC with the rest of your family, or shuttling between devices with USB drives. Today, we all access multiple devices—smartphones, tablets, computers, and Chromebooks, and we need a means of accessing each of these devices without necessarily moving around.

The RPI2 is one powerful device that you can play around with to build your own cloud, where you can have family pictures and documents. To do this, consider attaching an external hard disk to your PI; you'll need the extra disk space to store your files: pictures, documents, movies, and TV shows.

10. Building a talking toy

The RPI2 is a good accessory for you if you want to build a talking toy or chatter telephone. You can then give it additional functionality; think of how you can configure your talking toy to tell you the current time, breaking news, local weather updates, traffic updates, sports scores and fixtures, stock exchange rates, and much more. There are numerous fun features that you can easily exploit with your RPI2 device.

11. Building a PI Microwave

Think of a raspberry pie cooked on a Raspberry Pi. This would never come to be without a Pi microwave (call it picrowave). Why not build an entire microwave on your own?

There's nothing you can't build on your Raspberry Pi, not even a microwave. You don't have to start off from scratch; you can grab a few components from your old microwave and figure how you can hook them up to your Pi.

You don't want to rebuild your old model, but to build an improved version of your old microwave. Here are a few things to consider incorporating into your picrowave:

o   Softer sounds

o   Redesigned-touchpad

o   Auto-clock

o   Voice-control

o   Wi-Fi control

o   Bluetooth control

o   App-control

12. Building a Pi security camera

If you are really into modern electronics, you'll not be satisfied with constructing a simple RPi2 media center. Setting up a Pi CCTV camera is something you would want to try; think of building a real surveillance system that you can rely on to take clear footage and captivating photos.

To turn your PI into a security camera, you don't need much: all you need is your Pi, SD card, Ethernet connection, a camera module, and a few easy to install add-ons. To start you off, install MotionPie (security suite) on your RPI2. The end product of your setup will be a surveillance system that's capable of detecting motion, broadcasting live streams, and much more.

With the application, you'll be able to secure your network, adjust resolution, capture video motion, and a lot more. MotionPie refers to a camera-viewing application that works like a typical IP camera.

13. Building a wearable computer

Given the small size of the RPI2, conceiving it as some wearable computer (call it PiBerry eyewear) would not be completely out of the character of digital environment. Think of Google Glass powered by Pi. Based on this, you can actually come up with PiBerry eyewear that allows one to view immersive video content in the comfort of their bed, or from any other convenient spot.

Making Pi eyewear that can easily click onto other wearable displays would be a big plus. Including a mini-pocket keyboard or a voice control (microphone control) system would not be a stretch for such a powerful pocket gadget.

14. Building a PiBeacon

You have definitely heard about Apple's iBeacons and BLE technology. Apple uses its iBeacons to broadcast advertisement messages to iOS 7 devices within their range. With a slight idea of how the protocol works, hackers can venture out to build their own Raspberry Pi beacons and transmit messages to Android devices within range.

Wouldn't this be fun? For more fun, simply tag your car with a BLE tag and receive an instant alert when that car moves out of range. You'll of course need your RPI2, a micro SD card, a USB Bluetooth dongle (4.0 standard), and a beacon toolkit from Apple store for testing purposes. Once set up, a working PiBeacon will be able to transmit messages (advertising data) if it discovers your phone within its range.

This is a great idea for business persons who wish to customize their retail offers depending on their geographical location or proximity to their products.

15. Building a 3D scanner

Based on the RPI2 device, you can build a complete 3D scanner at a very low cost. This would largely benefit archaeologists and medical practitioners in need of accurate on-the-spot scans. For a perfect 3D scan, you'll need something that can capture a 360-degree image. You can borrow a few ideas from Microsoft's Kinect and many others out there.

16. Building a touch screen dashboard

With a little effort and determination, you can build a touch screen dashboard for your car or any other device using your RPi2. If you were to buy a working dashboard for your car, off-the-shelf, you'll obviously not smile at the price. Using the XBMC software as previously mentioned, your dashboard should respond to touch, and allow you play music, browse your photos, and watch your videos.

17. Building a Minecraft server

Your tiny RPI2 device can be transformed into a low-cost Minecraft server that offers greater multiplayer control than what most public servers would offer. This would be much cheaper than having a private server on a remote network.

18.Creating a digital Pi photo frame

Raspberry Pi allows you to build a digital picture frame with much better features than what you'll get at a local store. Other than just displaying photos, you can use the RPI2 picture frame to display weather reports, movies, music, and much more.

19.Building a Pi mobile robot

With the RPI2 board, you don't need a huge investment to build a mobile robot. You can actually build a remote-controlled robot powered by a Raspberry Pi for less than $200. You'll however need a few other compatible components, like a USB power hub and Wi-Fi router to give your robot some life.

20. Building a landline

If you have development skills, you wouldn't want to spend any more on a landline if you own the RPI2. It's very possible to replace the Google Voice with Pi, and start making free calls straightaway. You can use your smartphones for emergency calls.

21.Building a miniature balloon

A miniature balloon is a familiar term for enthusiasts who fancy the space. Miniature ballooning allows such individuals to have a view of the world from high altitudes above the sky. You can build such a balloon that's powered by the Raspberry Pi 2 that you just acquired, and grab breathtaking shots of the world using a miniature camera hooked on the balloon.

22.Building a Pi drone

Use the RPI2 board to build a remote-controlled Raspberry Pi drone for use at home. Think of how you can make your drone fly on autopilot. With a map as the only input to your Pi drone, the drone should be able to trace its own perfect path with the help of the GPRS.

23.Building a Pi book player

The Rpi2 board comes standard with an audio port and micro SD card slot, which makes it perfect for building an audiobook player. This implies that you can a one-button player capable of reading out your books loud. Audiobook readers are a good invention for the visually impaired.

24.Building a coffee machine

How can it feel like starting a coffee machine with some command? The RPi2 board is what you need to build such commands, and many others for your kitchen appliances. You'll however need some input and output controller to effectively monitor your coffee machine.

25.Building a board for analog input

The RPi2 board comes with 40 GPIO pins that allow you to hook up your Pi with additional components. Unfortunately, these pins do not support analog inputs, a good reason for you to build an analog board that will allow for such connections. Think of how you can convert analog signals to digital signals.

Chapter 4 – Expansion Boards for Raspberry Pi 2

The Raspberry Pi 2 board is the latest release, and comes chock-a-block full with powerful features, among them 1 GB RAM and 900 MHz processor. Because of its great power and speed, the market has been flooded with great miscellanea of accessories in an attempt to get the most out of this Pi board. The most popular expansion add-ons include:

Pi Lite

Pi Lite refers to a large multi-purpose LED matrix board that clicks onto the GPIO pins of the Rpi2. This display features a total of 126 LEDs largely used to scroll graphics and texts.

It's a 9x14 display board that comes with an onboard processor and a GPIO connector. The Pi Lite illustrates how your RP2 can be used to create fun and physical projects. Every single pixel on the display can be addressed individually through its serial port, allowing you to display whatever you want on the grid. You don't even have to solder it to your Pi; simply plug the board into your Pi.

One huge advantage of this matrix is that it doesn't draw power from the Pi, but from its ATMega328p processor, freeing the Pi of overload.

PiFace Real Time Clock

The PiFace Clock is a board designed to ensure that your RPi2 keeps time at all times even when offline. The good thing about the PiFace device is its invisible nature and ability to fit onto the GPIO pins, while still sparing enough room to fit other compatible accessories. With this add-on, your RPi2 always shows the right time regardless of its position. It still works even in the absence of a working Internet.

PiFace Digital

PiFace digital is another great board that you can add to your Pi. With this board, you can hook up your RPi2 with devices such as motors, switches, and lights. This implies that you'll be able to tell when specific buttons are pressed, doors are opened, switches are closed, or when circuits are touched off. You will also be able to use your RPi2 to flash lights, spin motors, sound horns, wink LEDs, and do much more.

PiFace Control and Display

This device presents you with status information regarding your Pi. If you have this board hooked to your Pi, you might not need a monitor or keyboard for your RPi2—the device comes with some infrared receiver and navigation switch, which preempt the need for traditional input devices.

RasPi Robot V2

The RasPi Robot expansion board is a perfect add-on for tinkerers who would like to turn their RPi2 boards into motor controllers. It comes when fully assembled with its own power supply, and easily fits over the GPIO pins of your Pi.

Chapter 5 – Troubleshooting

Though small in size, handling your RPi2 may present a couple issues, some pretty easy to resolve, and others passably complex. The more composite your device, the more complex its issues can get. Fortunately, most of the problems you will encounter can be easily diagnosed and fixed with significant ease and comfort. In this section, we focus on the issues that you are most likely to encounter with your RPi2 and the most effective solutions to those particular problems.

Xenon flash glitch

Users of the RPi2 board are likely to experience hardware reboot issues when taking photos of their newly acquired Pi. This is because the Pi's core switch is camera-shy. The fix to this problem is pretty simple; don't use a camera flash, and if you really have to use it, just make sure it's not a xenon flash. Alternatively, finding a Pi case for your device would be a quick fix.

Display diagnostics

Your RPi2 should work with HDMI, DVI, and composite video, but this may not always be the case when you attach these display devices to your Pi. Occasionally, your pictures may shift to one side of the display, appear distorted, or even not appear at all. In some cases, your HDMI may not display anything, or if it does, the resolution may not be the best.

Most issues with the monitor are fixed by changing the "config.txt" file. Be sure to back up the file before continuing. You'll have to type a few commands to see your current display settings, supported display modes, and the preferred settings.

Boot diagnostics

Your Pi won't boot? If your RPi2 fails to boot when powered on, the problem is most likely with the micro SD card. To boot successfully, the Pi communicates with the files written on the micro SD card, and when the files are corrupted, the entire operation aborts. If the power light of your RPi2 glows, but nothing shows up on the screen, then you'll have to replace your card with a compatible one. You'll also want to be sure that the micro-USB cable is well suited for your Pi.

Your RPi2 will not read the contents of your SD card if you are not using a stable, fit-for-purpose power supply unit. If you are attempting to boot your pi on an older disk image, it will also not work. While switching off your RPi2, don't simply pull out the SD card; doing so, slowly damages your card.

Input diagnostics

One other problem that you may experience with your RPi2 is repeated characters on your screen when you press on your keyboard or move your mouse. One reason for that could be a power overload on the Pi; this occurs when your input device—keyboard or mouse—draws immense power from the RPi2. The USB ports on the Pi have a polyfuse component that trips when a device consumes too much power from it. To fix the issue, connect your USB mouse or keyboard to the RPi2 via a USB power hub.

Network diagnostics

If your Pi is connected to a home router via say the Ethernet, but you still can't connect to the Internet, you can fix the issue using the "ifconfig" tool. **ifconfig** is superb for configuring and controlling the network ports of your RPi2. Run this tool to get all the information you need on the network ports of your Pi.

Power diagnostics

When you power on your RPi2, the red LED that indicates power status should consistently stay red. If this is not case, or the LED does not even light at all, then there's a problem with your power connection. A blinking red LED is a pointer to a bad power supply unit. In this case, you need to change your power supply unit.

If the green LED doesn't flash when the micro SD card is plugged in to your RPi2, it implies a missing system image or a corrupted one. If the Pi can't locate a valid system image, the green LED glows steadily, but remains faint. Check to confirm that   the   card   is   installed   correctly.

Conclusion

The Raspberry Pi 2 board is the perfect solution for every project you can possibly think of today in the world of modern electronics. The first 26 GPIO pins of the RPi2 board offer support to all expansion boards and other third-party add-ons designed to work with previous RPi models.

Given its massive power and memory, you can rely on this single-board computer to create any project of your choice for educational use, commercial use, or even for fun. This guideline should be used together with other guidelines and tutorials to get the ultimate experience with your Raspberry Pi 2 board.

When you master the basics discussed in this guideline, you'll be able to build your own fun projects.

www.ingramcontent.com/pod-product-compliance
Lightning Source LLC
LaVergne TN
LVHW052324060326
832902LV00023B/4595